LEVEL TWO

chords
and keys

for individual or group instruction

multi-keys

By **Mary Elizabeth Clark**
and **David Carr Glover**

David Carr Glover
PIANO LIBRARY

Foreword

This book is written especially for Group Piano Instruction. However, it can be used to much advantage in the individual lesson. The students should have had the equivalent of the Primer and Level One of the DAVID CARR GLOVER PIANO LIBRARY, including CHORDS AND KEYS, Level One. The students should have played tunes in all Major Keys and know the I and V7 chords.

This book gives the students interesting music in all fifteen Major Keys using I, IV, and the V7 chords. The page preceding each piece gives the patterns used in the piece. In many cases the melody hand must make one or two shifts. When the students transpose the pieces, they are transposing by intervals and direction as well as finger numbers.

It is important that the teacher have the students discover the common tones of the chords and the whole and half-step movement of the chord progression.

A word about Group Piano Instruction:

The teacher of Group Piano is more than a piano instructor; he is a teacher of MUSIC.

The advantages of Group Piano Instruction over the individual lesson are numerous. The students study a much broader curriculum. They discover and learn concepts of music. They have opportunities to create and improvise and acquire the tools needed for these activities. They become independent in their study and do not lean upon the teacher to do their thinking and planning for them. Students learn the fundamentals of music thoroughly and enjoyably because they are sharing with each other. They become acquainted with a broad cross-section of music literature through music appreciation and hearing their classmates perform music other than what each is studying. For example, if a certain composer is being studied, part of the group can learn one piece and part of the group another piece by this composer, and they all benefit from hearing and studying the structure and interpretation of every piece learned by the group.

Students in a group must play the rhythm correctly in order to participate. Reasons for correct rhythm and other music fundamentals are very apparent to these students. The students teach each other.

Any problems of group teaching for the teacher can be met with good planning, well in advance, and adequate equipment. The equipment need not be elaborate, but it must be practical.

Discipline problems are few if the students are kept busy every minute of the lesson and a change of pace takes place every few minutes. The inexperienced group teacher must guard against the students getting the upper hand. This is usually caused by enthusiasm out of control. This spirit is not to be dampened, but led and guided by the teacher.

Attendance by parents at the lesson part of the time is to be encouraged. Parents are informed and understand how to help at home. The interest of parents often leads to adult study. Adult groups can meet at times other than "prime time" on the teacher's schedule and contribute to the teacher's resources.

Group instruction enables the teacher to teach more students in the time available and with a higher quality of instruction than in individual lessons.

Differences in abilities will exist within any group. Some students learn more quickly in some areas while others learn more quickly in other areas. The strong points and weak points of the members of a group usually balance out. The faster learning students should learn more material of the same level rather than move ahead of the group.

A group of six students is easily handled in the private studio. This allows for one or two group changes leaving a minimum of four. Six students can be taught at two pianos. Two students are at the pianos, two are observing, and two are at tables or behind the pianos with practice keyboards on top of the pianos. Many times there are two students at each piano, with two observing. A traffic pattern should be developed so that the students move about easily. Some writing work can be done at every lesson allowing the teacher flexibility to work with one or two students for a few minutes.

A lesson time of fifty minutes is suggested if once a week, less if twice a week. Allowing an hour on the schedule with an actual fifty minutes of lesson time gives the students time to enter and leave the studio.

Rhythm instruments, flash cards, visual aids, record player, tape recorder, and other aids are very useful in group instruction.

There are many publications and articles out today on Group Instruction, as well as many Teacher's Workshops and Seminars. Workshops are presented by the authors of this book several times a year in major cities and on location in Virginia. Alert teachers will avail themselves of all this help and new materials.

THE DAVID CARR GLOVER

PIANO LIBRARY In Group Instruction:

The PIANO STUDENT and the PIANO THEORY, PRIMER, are used for the very first lessons. Many pieces in the STUDENT can be combined into ensembles. The PIANO REPERTOIRE book of the Primer Level may be introduced about the third lesson giving many more pieces. Numerous patterns are learned by memory at this time.

When the students progress into Level One, the PIANO STUDENT and CHORDS AND KEYS give the students a total learning experience of music reading and multi-keys. The same combination of books should continue in Level Two.

The PIANO THEORY, Level Two, should be used to correlate the fundamentals presented in the PIANO STUDENT. The PIANO REPERTOIRE provides additional music and the PIANO TECHNIC reinforces the technic elements presented in the STUDENT. The solo sheets of the LIBRARY provide the motivation and incentive for performance and pleasure.

Contents

Key of C Major

Patterns for BILL GROGAN'S GOAT

The melody of BILL GROGAN'S GOAT uses two positions of each hand.

RIGHT HAND

LEFT HAND

Chords used in BILL GROGAN'S GOAT. Practice hands separately.

C Chord

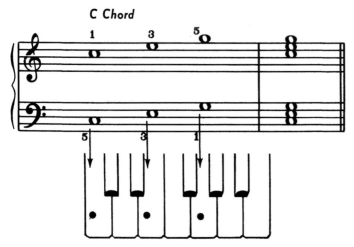

F Chord

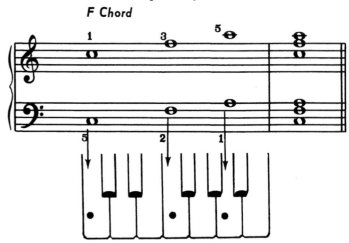

G7 Chord

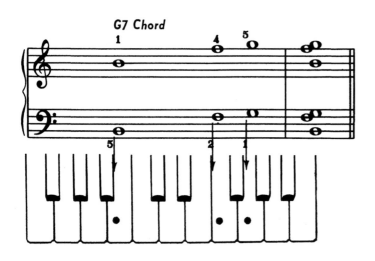

Memorize these chord patterns:

RIGHT HAND

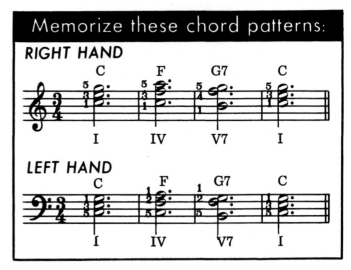

LEFT HAND

Write the Chords as indicated for the Key of C. Use whole notes.

Both hands.

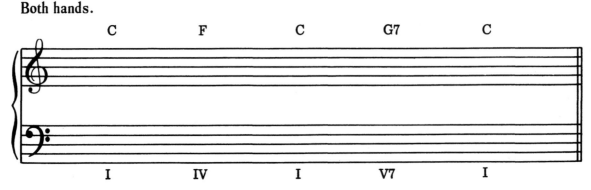

Bill Grogan's Goat

*The circled finger number indicates a move (position change) of the hand.

Key of F Major

Patterns for CRUISING

The melody of CRUISING uses only one position in each hand.

RIGHT HAND

LEFT HAND

Chords used in CRUISING. Practice hands separately.

F Chord

B♭ Chord

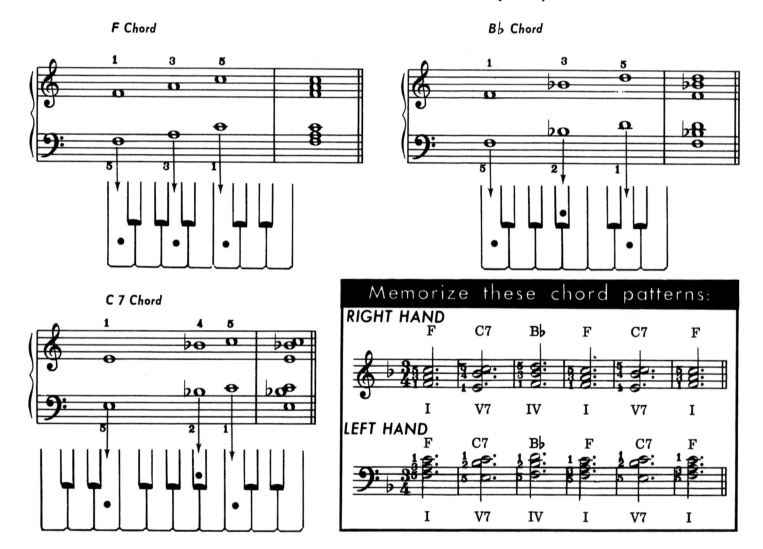

C 7 Chord

Memorize these chord patterns:

Write the Key Signature and the chords as indicated for the Key of F Major.
Use whole notes.

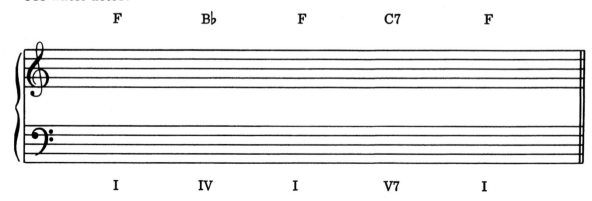

Cruising

CLARK

Key of B Flat Major

Patterns for APPLE PIE

The melody of APPLE PIE uses only one hand position in each hand.

RIGHT HAND

LEFT HAND

Chords used in APPLE PIE. Practice hands separately.

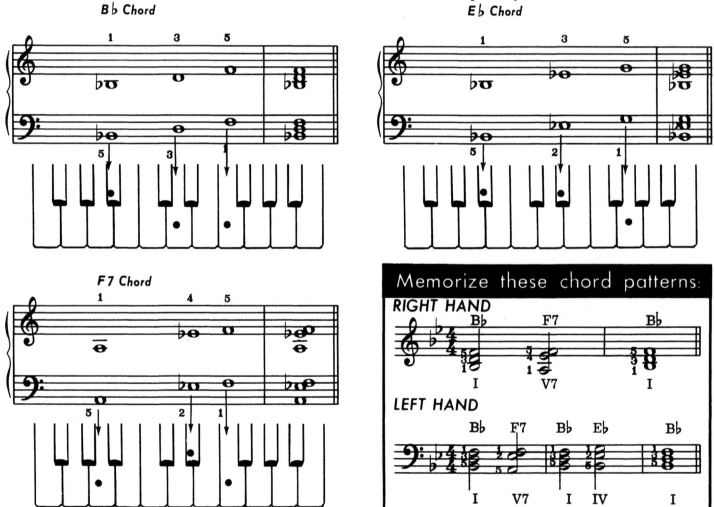

Write the Key Signature and the chords as indicated for the Key of B flat Major.
Use whole notes.

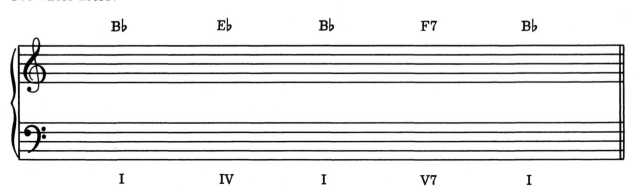

Apple Pie

GLOVER

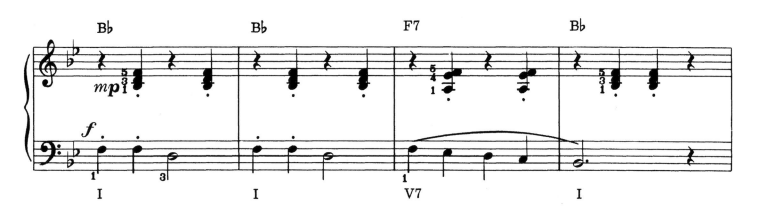

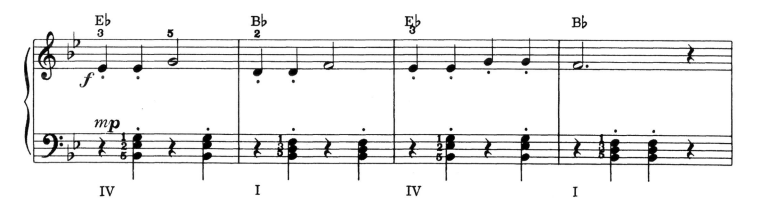

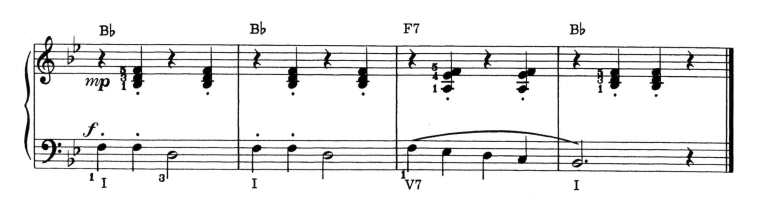

Key of E Flat Major

Patterns for FIDDLE-DEE-DEE

The melody of FIDDLE-DEE-DEE uses two
positions of the right hand.

RIGHT HAND

Pattern 1.

Pattern 2.

Chords used in FIDDLE-DEE-DEE. Practice the right hands chords, too, so
that you will know them for transposing pieces that use right hand chords.

Eb Chord

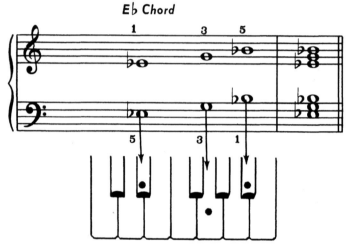

Ab Chord

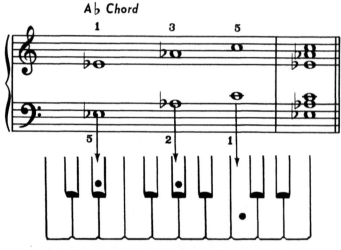

Bb7 Chord

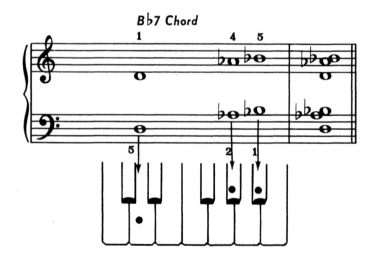

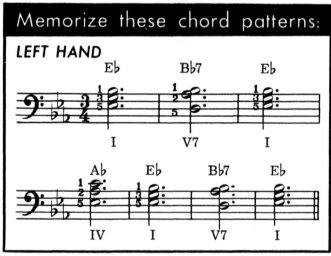

Memorize these chord patterns:

LEFT HAND

Write the Key Signature and chords as indicated for the Key of E flat Major.
Use whole notes.

Eb	Ab	Eb	Bb7	Eb

I   IV   I   V7   I

Fiddle-Dee-Dee

Key of A Flat Major

Patterns for CHERRIES RIPE

The melody of CHERRIES RIPE uses two positions of the right hand.

RIGHT HAND

Pattern 1.   Pattern 2.

Chords used in CHERRIES RIPE. Practice the right hand chords, too, so that you will know them for transposing pieces that use the right hand chords.

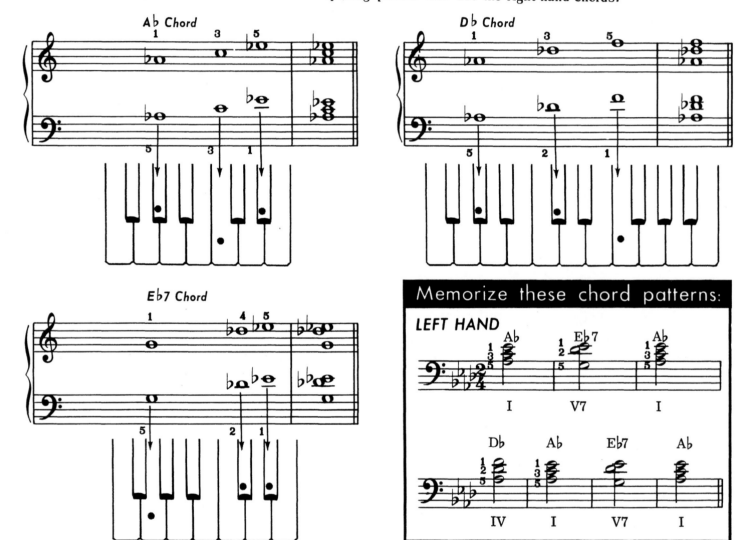

Write the Key Signature and chords as indicated for the Key of A flat Major.
Use whole notes.

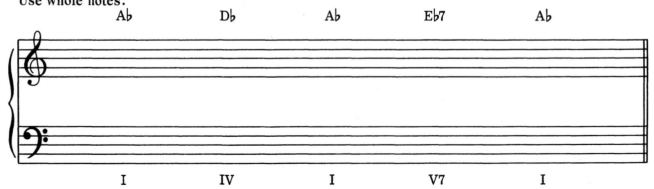

Cherries Ripe

Key of D Flat Major

Patterns for SWEET LEI LEHUA

RIGHT HAND

The melody of SWEET LEI LEHUA uses two positions of the right hand.

Chords used in SWEET LEI LEHUA. Practice hands separately.

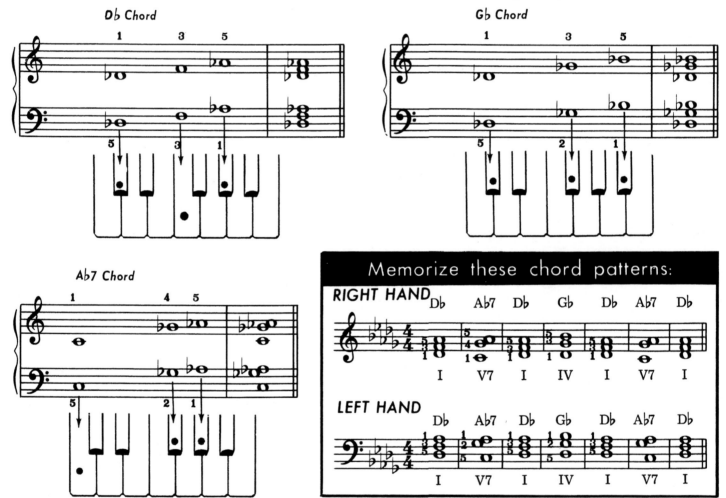

Write the Key Signature and the chords as indicated for the Key of D flat Major.
Use whole notes.

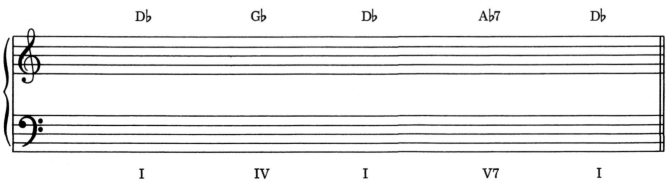

Sweet Lei Lehua

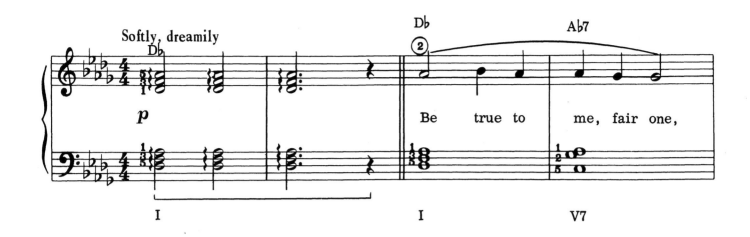

Softly, dreamily

Db   Db   Ab7

p

I   I   V7

Be true to   me, fair one,

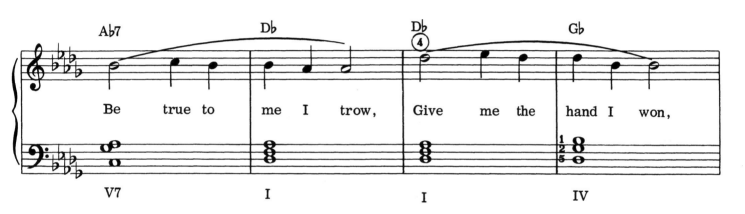

Ab7   Db   Db   Gb

Be true to   me I trow,   Give   me the   hand I   won,

V7   I   I   IV

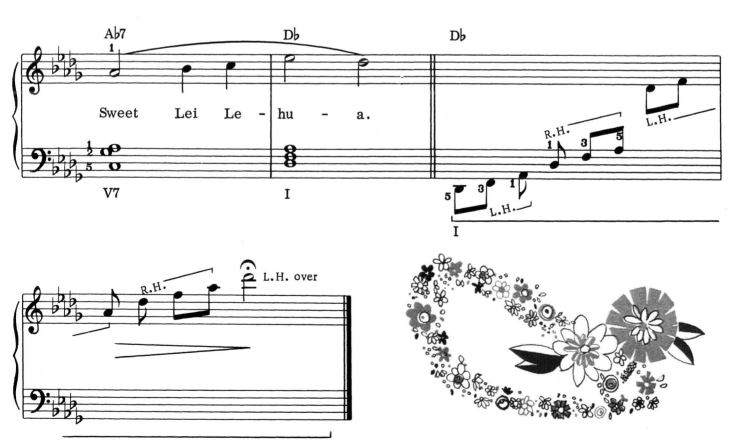

Ab7   Db   Db

Sweet   Lei Le - hu - a.

V7   I

I

R.H.

L.H.

L.H.

R.H.   L.H. over

Key of G Flat Major

Patterns for THE MAGNOLIA TREE

RIGHT HAND

The melody of the MAGNOLIA TREE uses only one position in the right hand.

Chords used in THE MAGNOLIA TREE. Practice the right hand chords, too, so that you will know them for transposing pieces that use the right hand chords.

Gb Chord

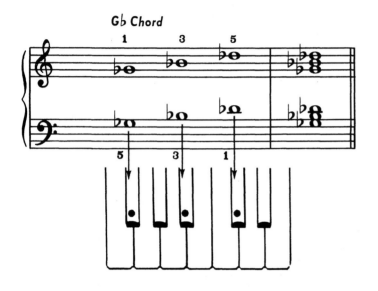

Cb Chord

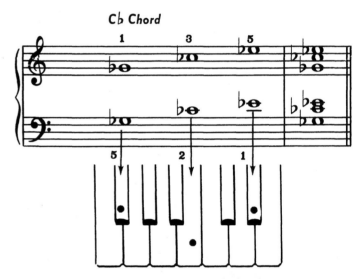

Db7 Chord

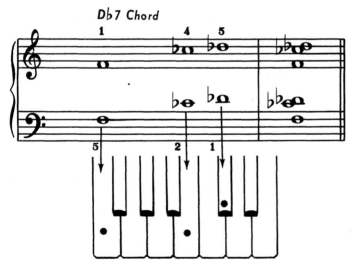

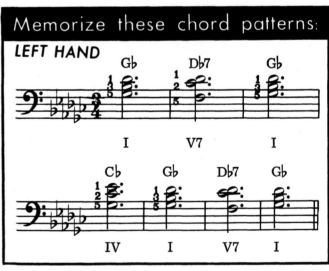

Write the Key Signature and chords as indicated for the Key of G flat Major.
Use whole notes.

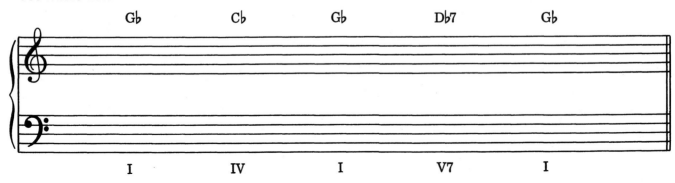

The Magnolia Tree

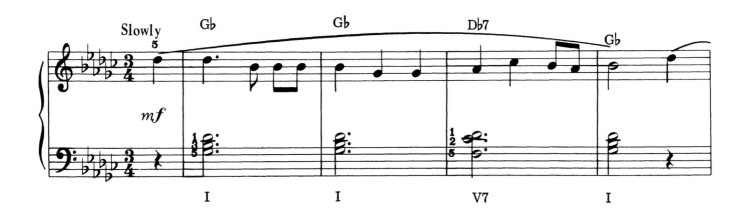

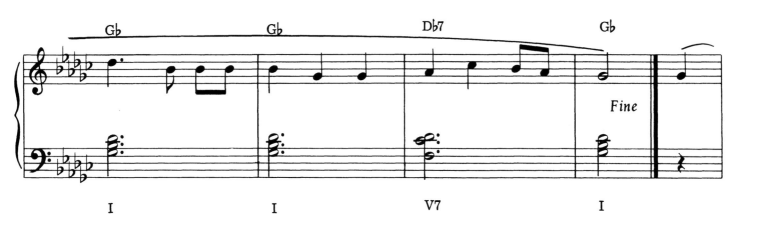

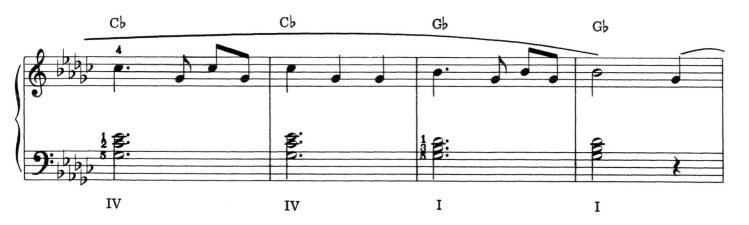

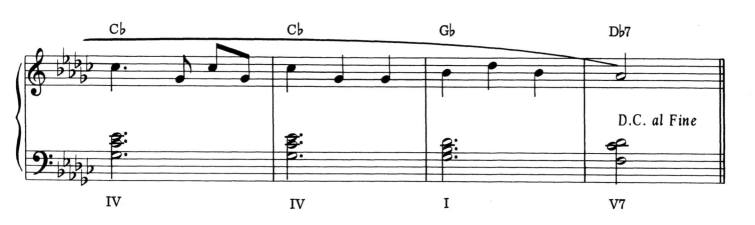

Key of C Flat Major

Patterns for THREE BLUE PIGEONS

The melody of THREE BLUE PIGEONS uses two positions and a scale extension in each hand.

Chords used in THREE BLUE PIGEONS. Practice hands separately.

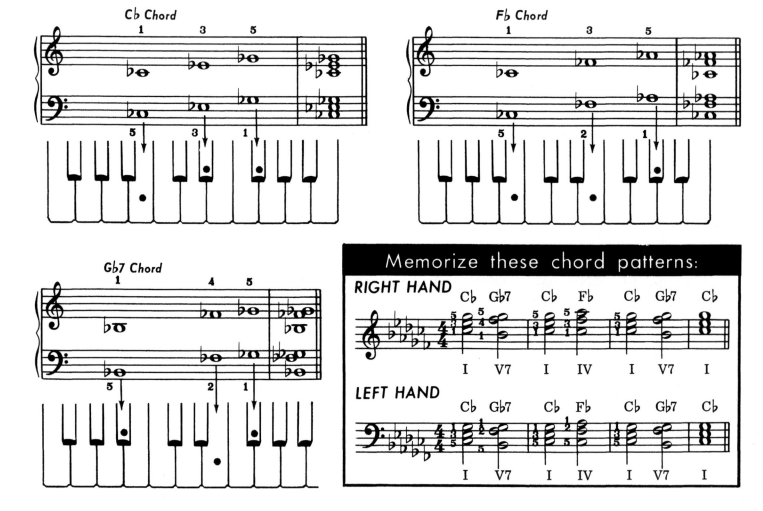

Write the Key Signature and chords as indicated for the Key of C flat Major.
Use whole notes.

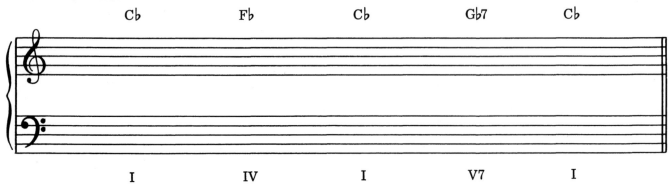

Three Blue Pigeons

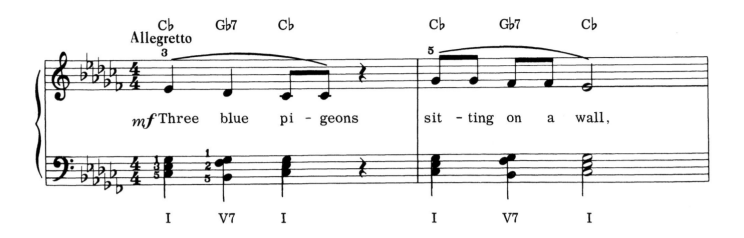

Three blue pi - geons sitting on a wall,

Three blue pi - geons sitting on a wall

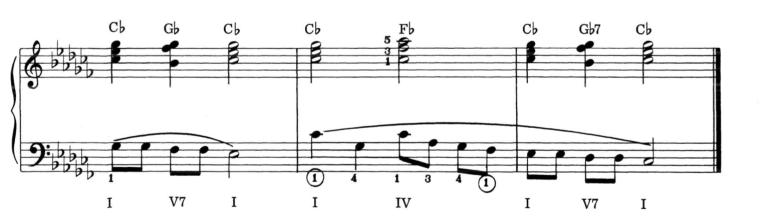

Key of C Sharp Major

Patterns for PEASE PORRIDGE HOT

The melody of PEASE PORRIDGE HOT uses two positions of each hand.

Chords used in PEASE PORRIDGE HOT. Practice hands separately.

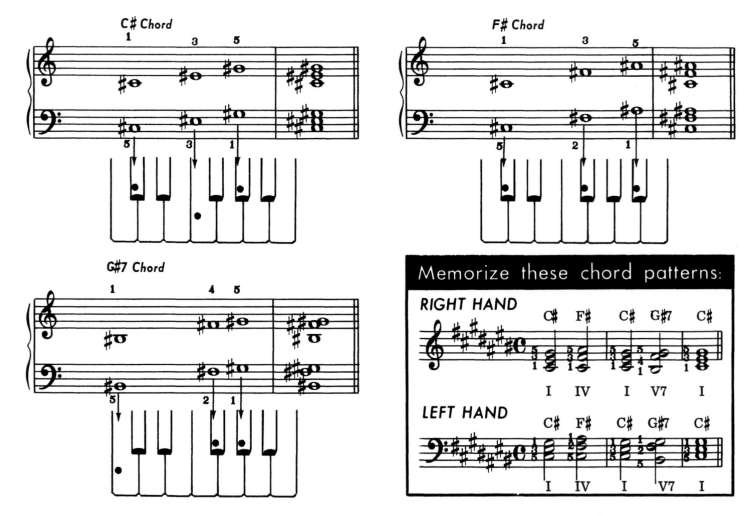

Write the Key Signature and the chords as indicated for the Key of C sharp Major.
Use whole notes.

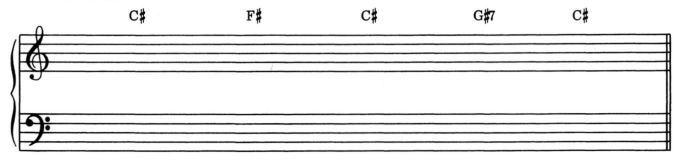

Pease Porridge Hot

Key of F Sharp Major

Patterns for LET'S GO A'HUNTING

RIGHT HAND

The melody of LET'S GO A'HUNTING uses only one hand position.

Chords used in LET'S GO A'HUNTING. Practice the right hand chords, too, so that you will know them for transposing pieces that use the right hand chords.

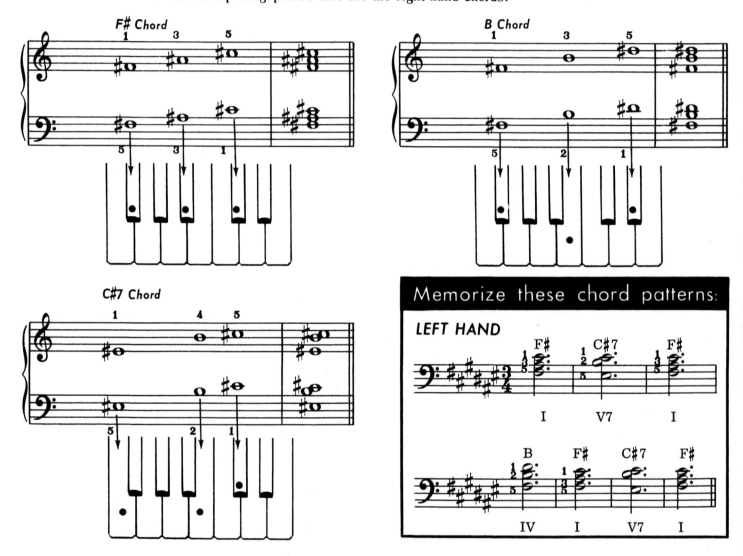

Write the Key Signature and the chords indicated for the Key of F sharp Major. Use whole notes.

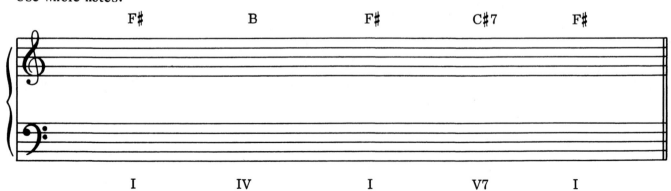

Let's Go A'Hunting

Key of B Major

Patterns for HUMMING TUNE

The melody of HUMMING TUNE uses two positions of the hands.

Chords used in HUMMING TUNE. Practice hands separately.

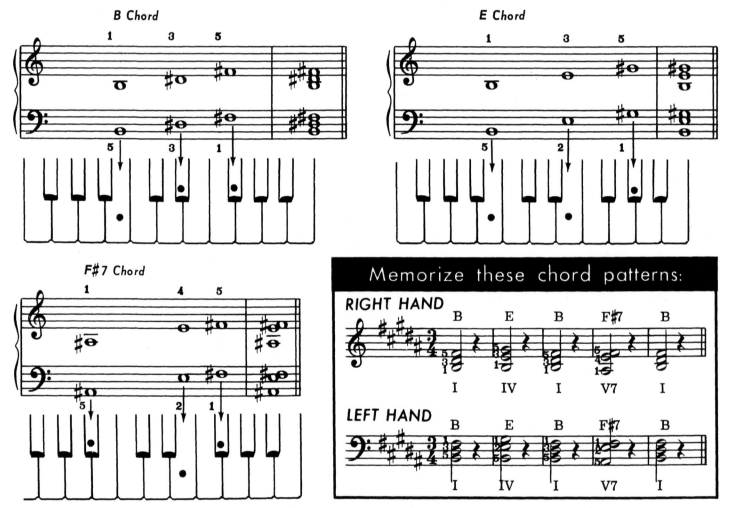

Write the Key Signature and the chords indicated for the Key of B Major.
Use whole notes.

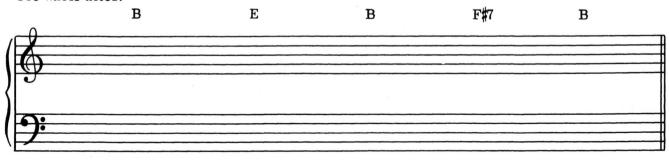

Humming Tune

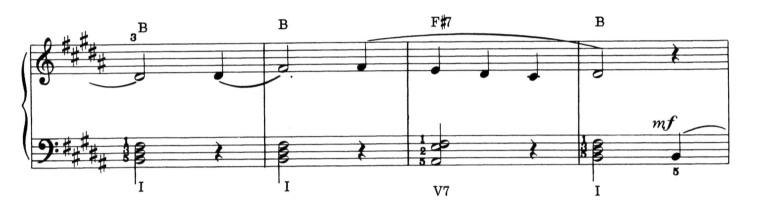

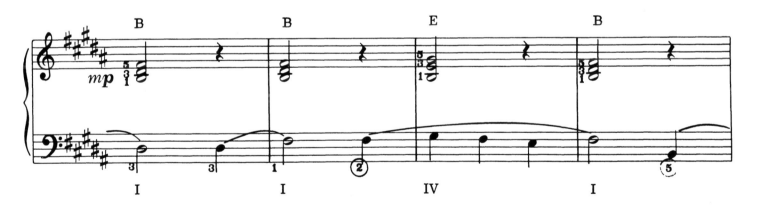

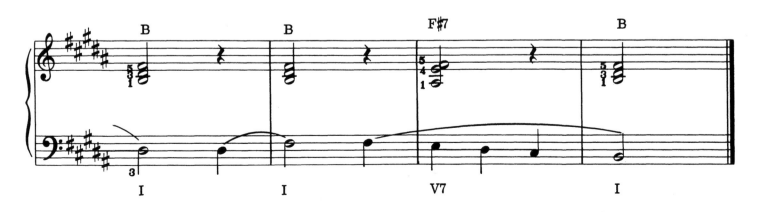

Patterns for MICHAEL, ROW THE BOAT ASHORE

RIGHT HAND

The melody of MICHAEL, ROW THE BOAT ASHORE uses two positions of the right hand.

Chords used in MICHAEL, ROW THE BOAT ASHORE. Practice the right hand chords, too, so that you will know them for transposing pieces that use the right hand chords.

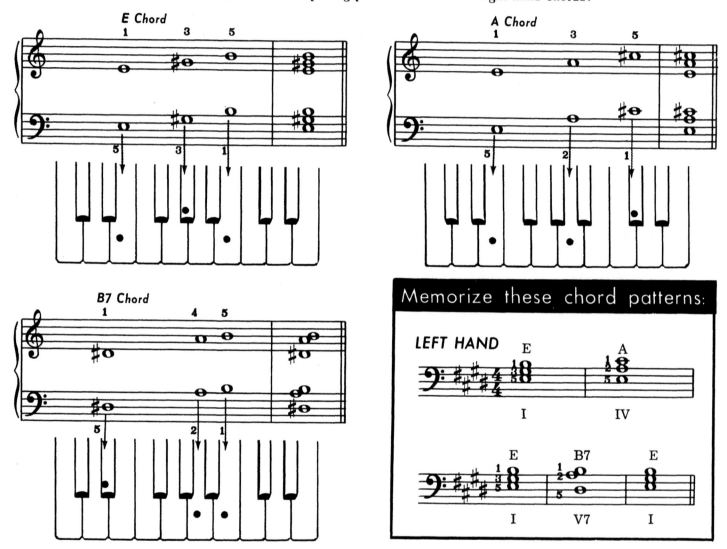

Write the Key Signature and the chords as indicated for the Key of E Major.
Use whole notes.

Michael, Row the Boat Ashore

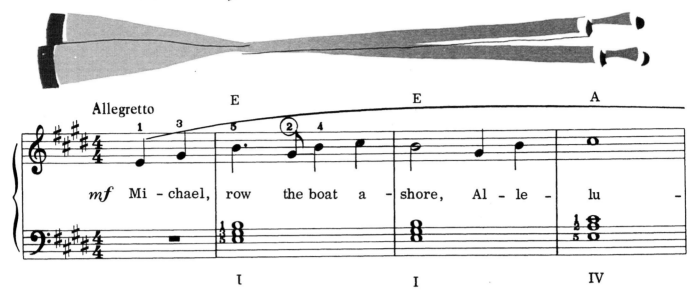

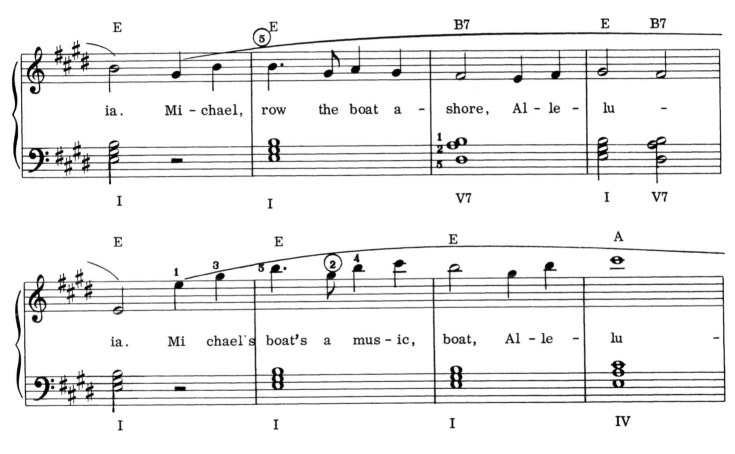

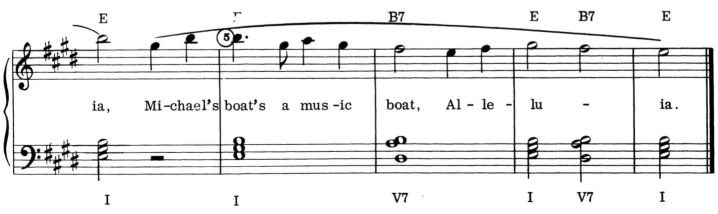

Key of A Major

Patterns for DUKE OF YORK

The melody of THE DUKE OF YORK uses only one position in each hand.

RIGHT HAND

LEFT HAND

Chords used in THE DUKE OF YORK. Practice hands separately.

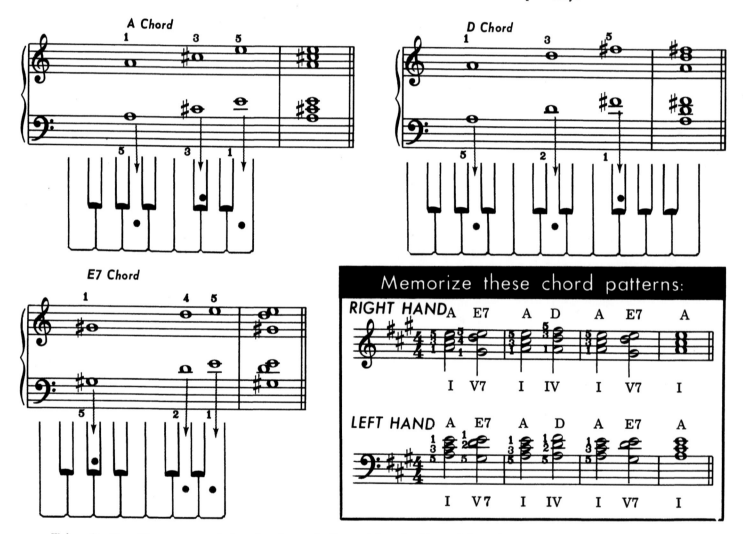

Write the Key Signature and the chords as indicated for the Key of A Major.
Use whole notes.

The Duke of York

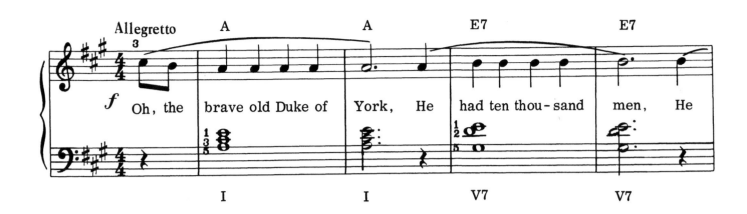

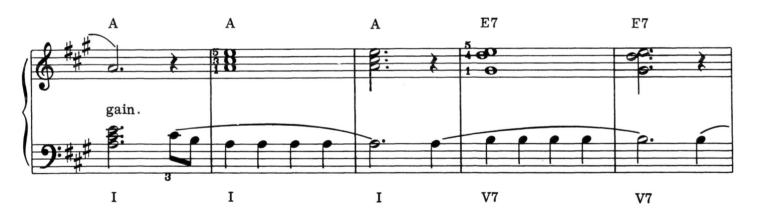

Key of D Major

Patterns for NELLY BLY

The melody of NELLY BLY uses two positions of each hand.

RIGHT HAND

LEFT HAND

Chords used in NELLY BLY. Practice hands separately.

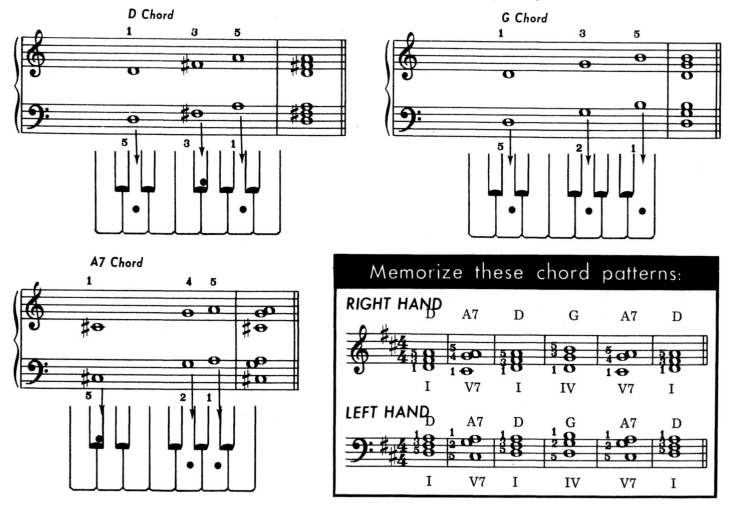

Write the Key Signature and the chords as indicated for the Key of D Major.
Use whole notes

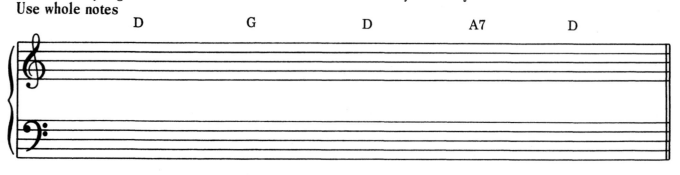

Nelly Bly

Foster

Moderato

Nel - ly Bly, Nel - ly Bly, bring the broom a - long, We'll

sweep the kitch -en clean, my dear, and have a lit - tle song.

Poke the wood, my la - dy love, and make the fire___ burn, And

while I take the ban - jo down, just give the mush a turn.

Patterns for LAVENDER'S BLUE

The melody of LAVENDER'S BLUE uses two
positions of the right hand.

LEFT HAND

Pattern 1   Pattern 2

Chords used in LAVENDER'S BLUE. Practice the right hand chords, too, so that
you will know them for transposing pieces that use the right hand chords.

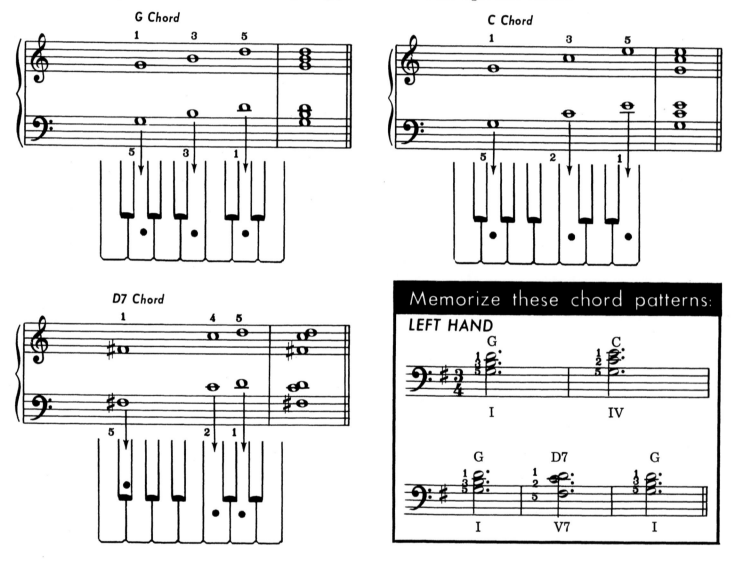

Write the Key Signature and the chords as indicated for the Key of G Major.
Use whole notes.

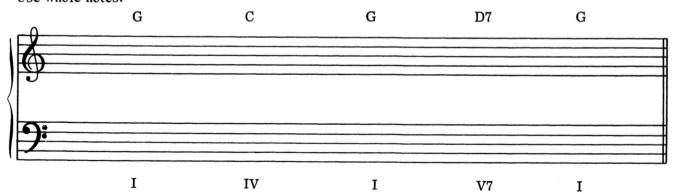

Lavender's Blue

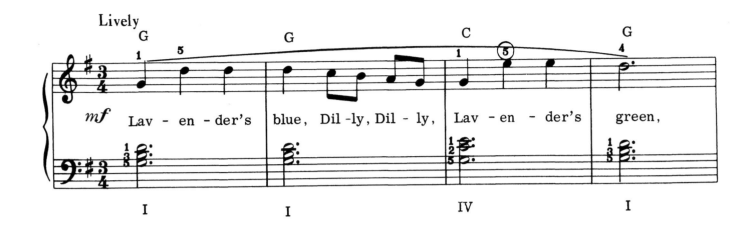

Lav - en -der's blue, Dil -ly, Dil - ly, Lav - en - der's green,

When I am King, Dil - ly, Dil - ly, you shall be Queen.

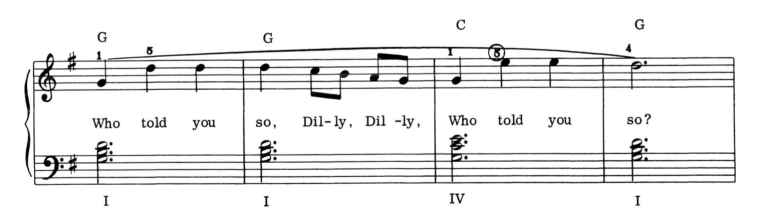

Who told you so, Dil - ly, Dil -ly, Who told you so?

'Twas my own heart, Dil - ly, Dil - ly, that told me so.

I IV V I Chords, Two Pianos, Eight Hands

Player 1

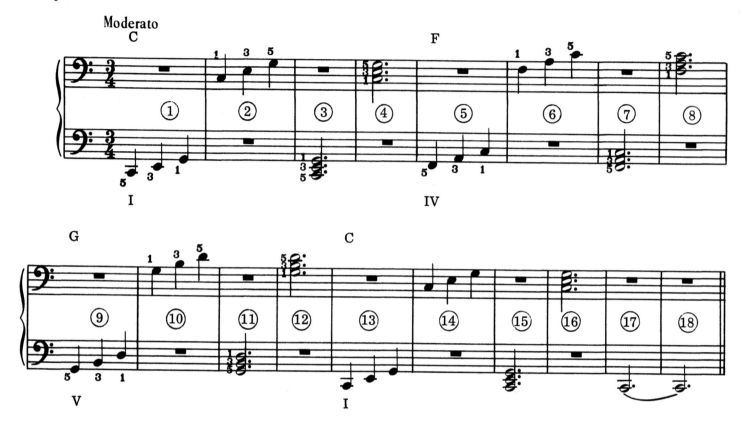

Player 3

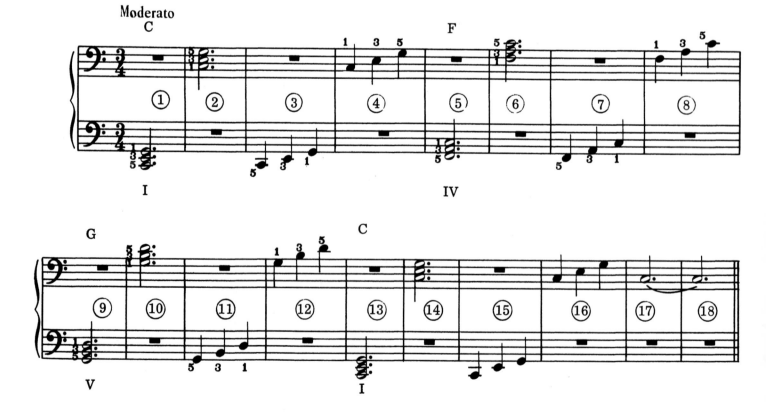

Transpose to other Major Keys.

I IV V I Chords, Two Pianos, Eight Hands*

Player 2

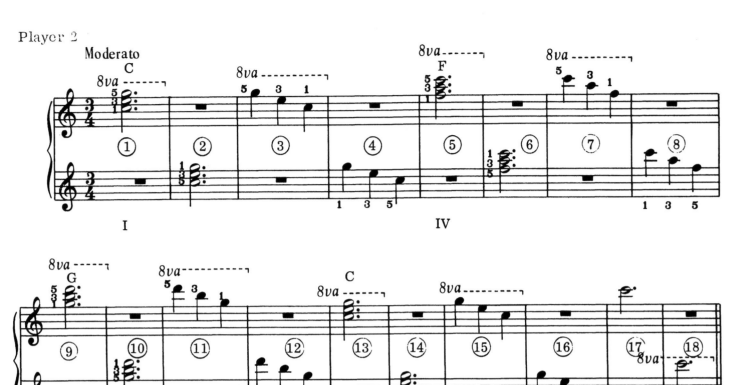

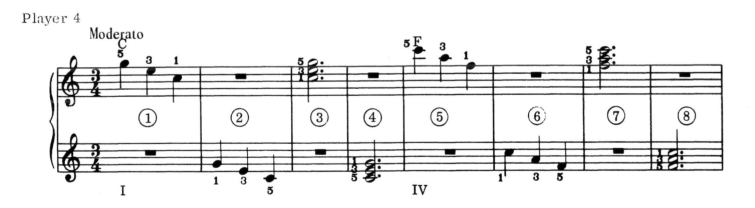

Player 4

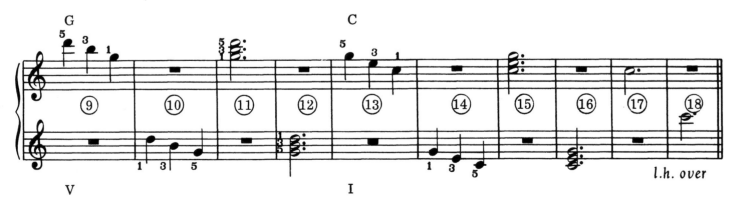

Any combination of these chord patterns may be used for ensemble. Players 1 and 2 may be played as a duet; also Players 3 and 4 may be played as a duet.

Peppermint Parade
Two Pianos, Eight Hands

Player 1

David Carr Glover

Peppermint Parade

Two Pianos, Eight Hands

David Carr Glover

Player 1

Player 3

Player 1

Player 3

Player 1

Player 3

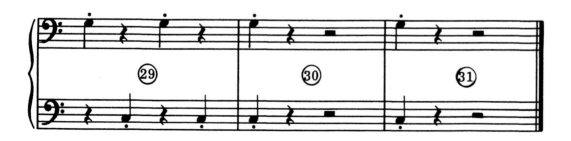

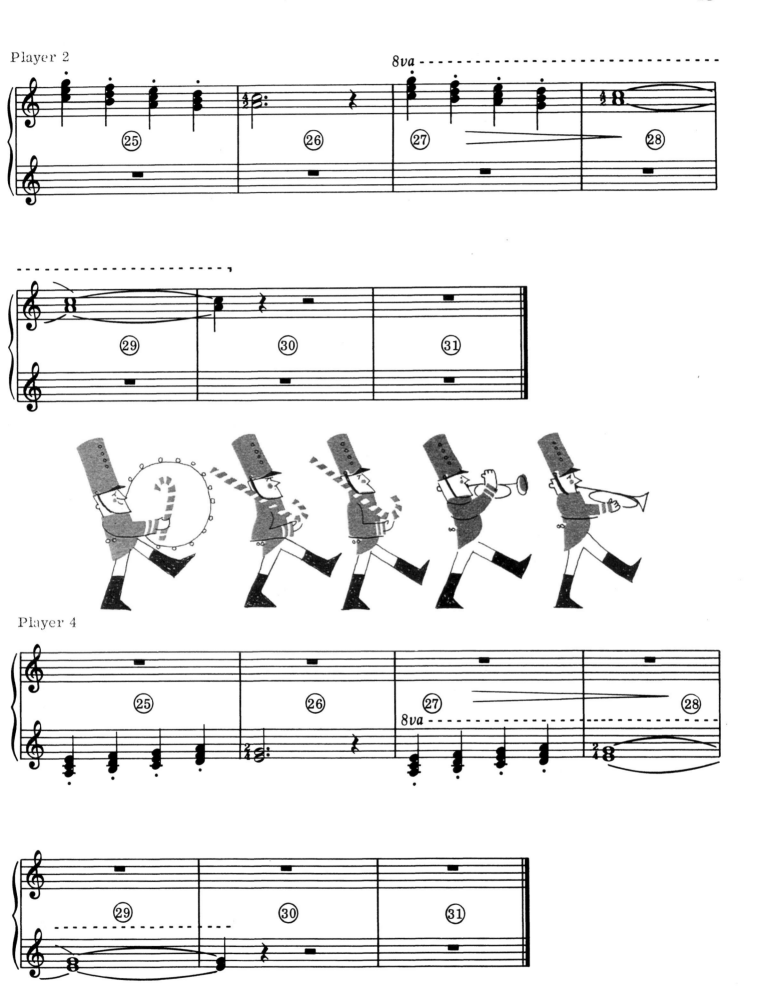

This piece can be played by any number of players from two on up, depending upon the number of instruments available. Players 1 and 2 can be used as a duet, as well as Players 3 and 4. Altogether they make a quartet.

An American Folk Song
(Ensemble)

CLARK

Player 1

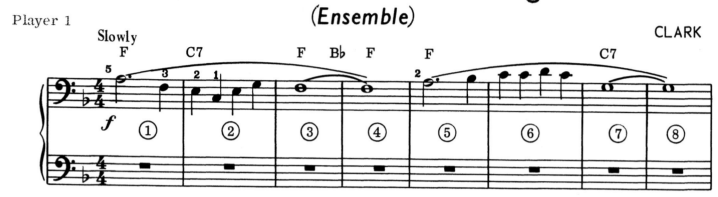

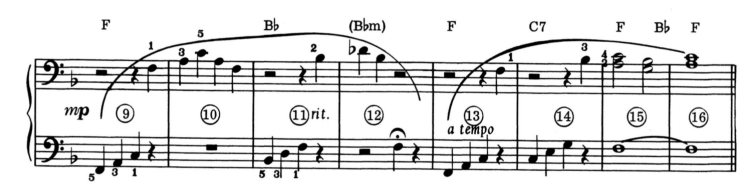

Player 3

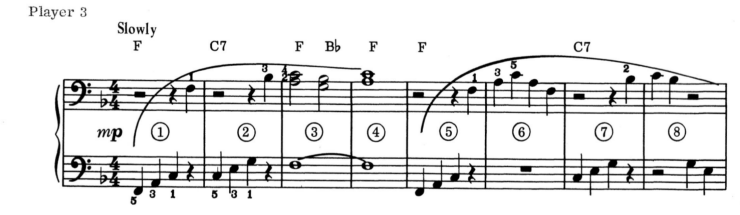

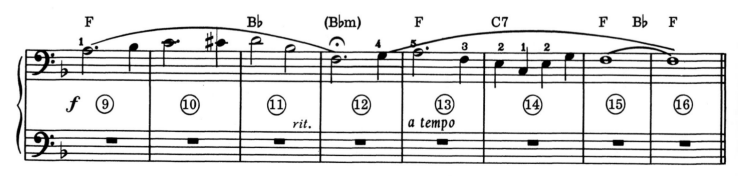

An American Folk Song
(Ensemble)

Player 2

CLARK

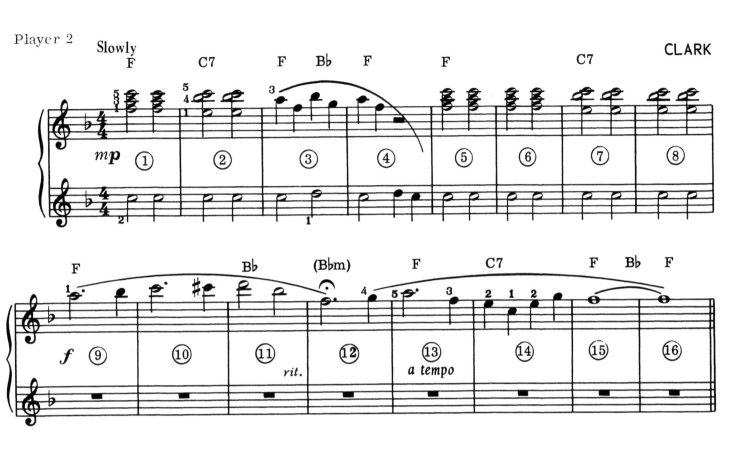

Player 4

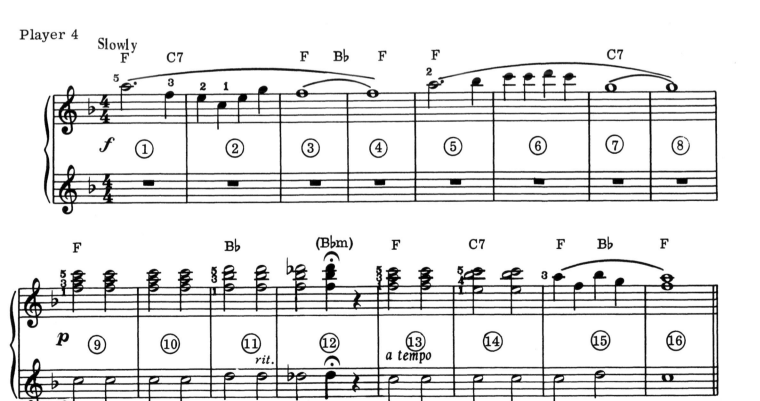

Chord Prelude
Two Pianos, Eight Hands

Glover

Player 1

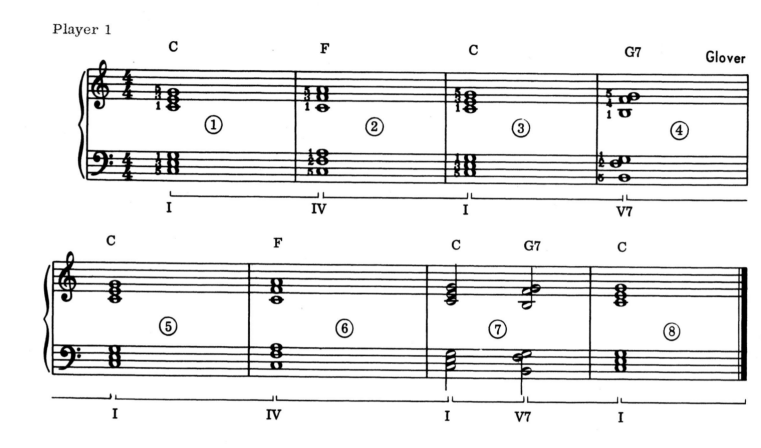

Player 3

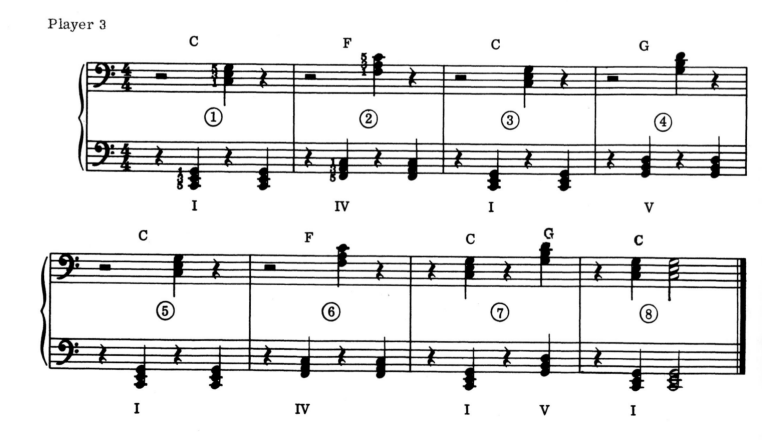

Chord Prelude
Two Pianos, Eight Hands

Player 2

Glover

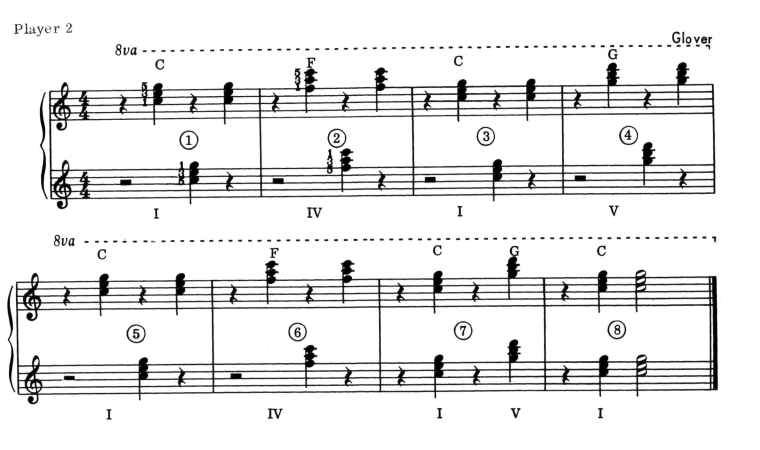

Player 4

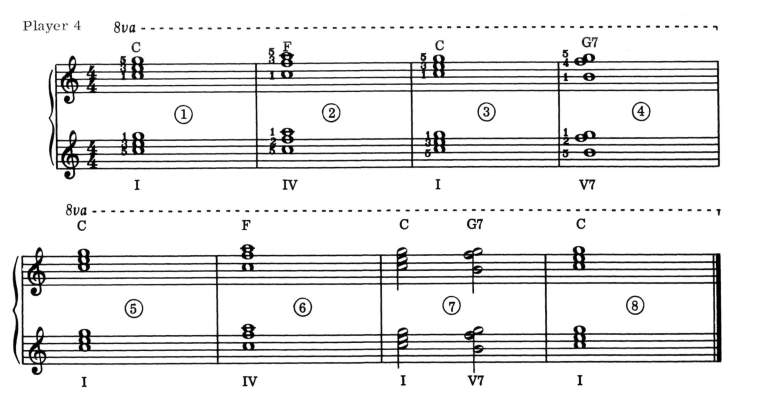

Warm-ups

To be transposed into all Major Keys when the Keys are studied.